Elk

Ring-necked pheasant

Grizzly bear

Canada goose

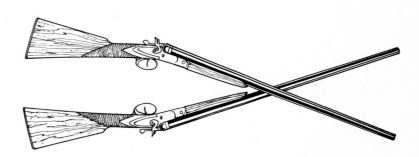

Red fox

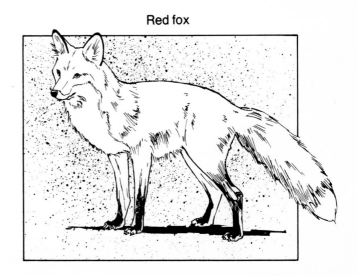

Bison

Mountain goat

5

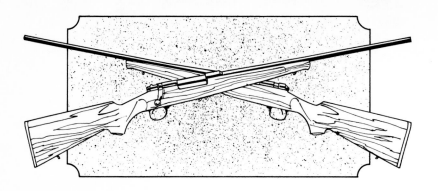

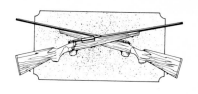

Squirrel

Ruffed grouse

Falcon

Setter

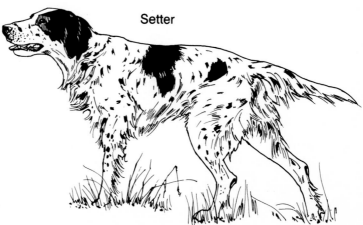

White-tailed deer

Bighorn sheep

Mountain lion

Turkey

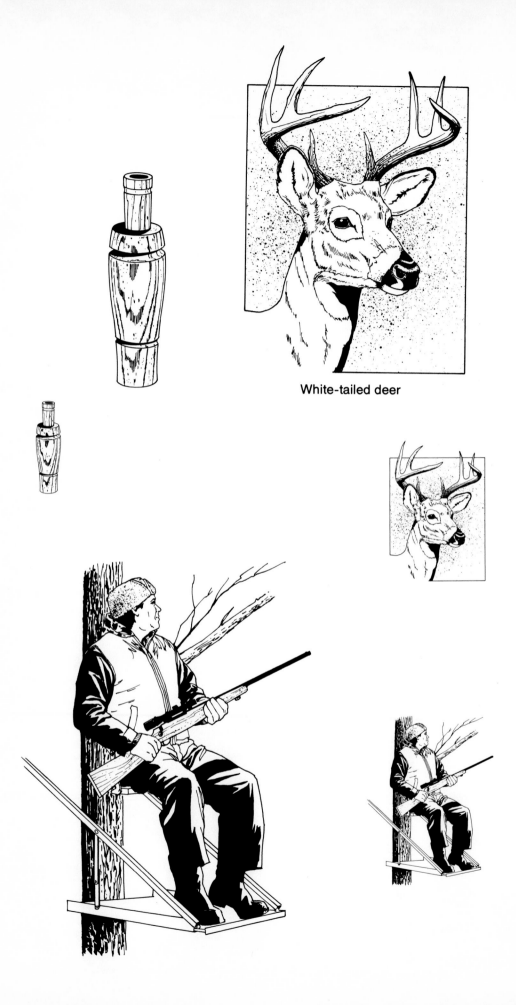

White-tailed deer

Pointer

Rabbit

Pronghorn

11

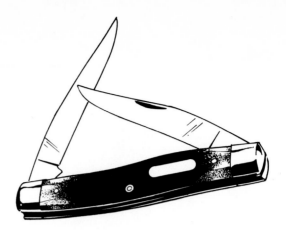

Moose

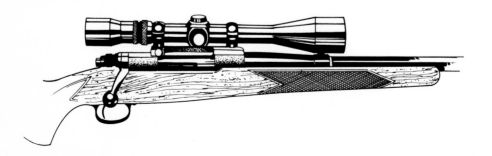

Rabbit

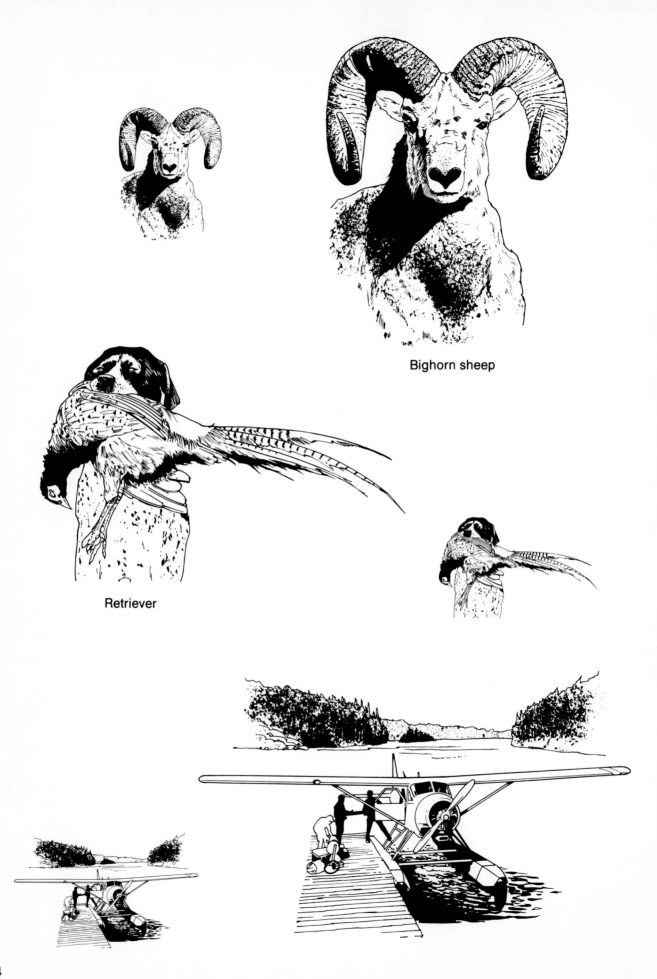

Bighorn sheep

Retriever

14

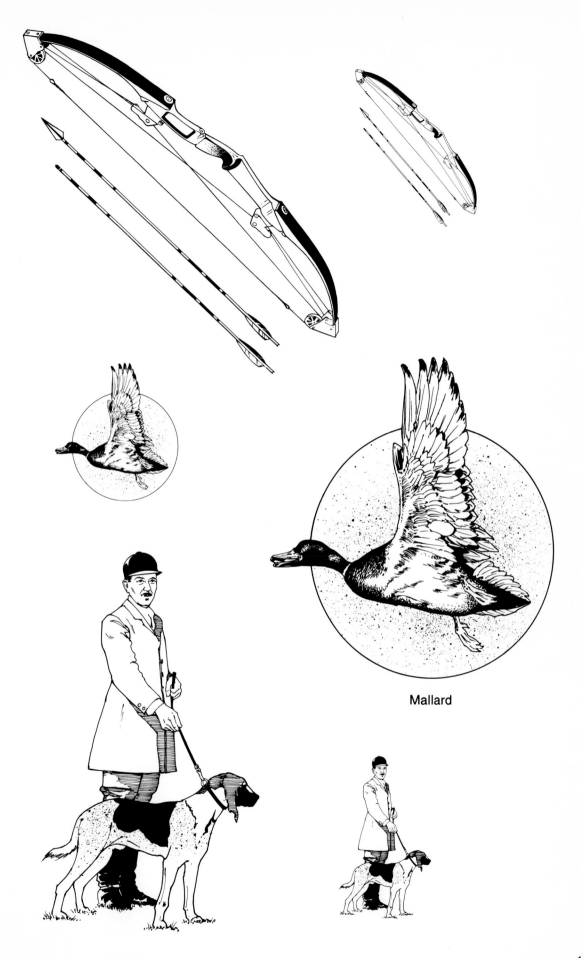

Mallard

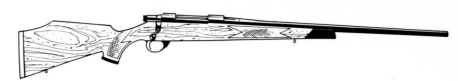

16

California Quail

Mule deer

Peccary

Turkey

Mallards, male (top) and female (bottom)

Caribou

Tuna

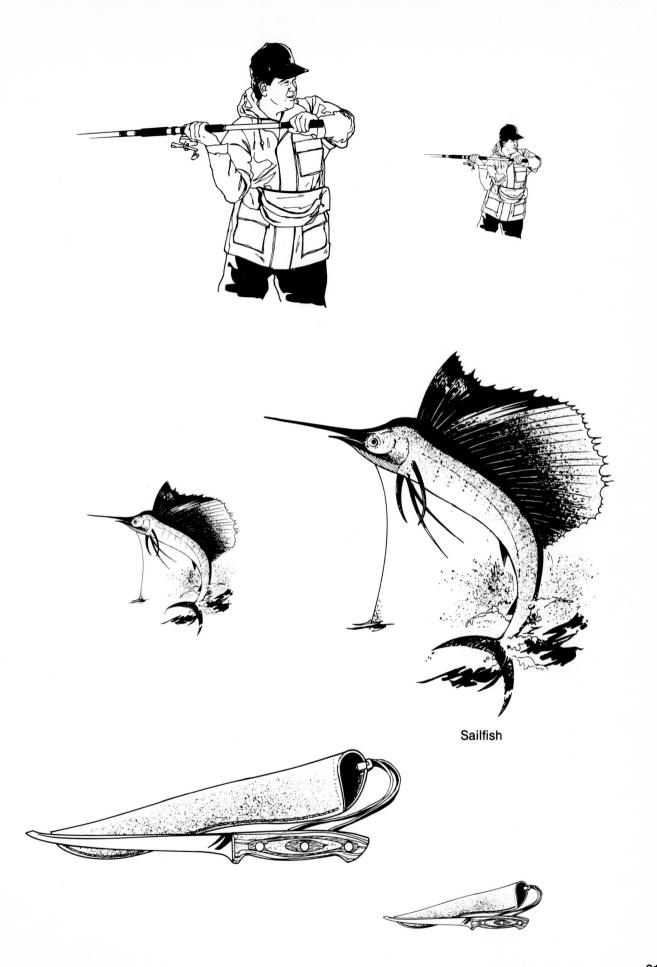

Sailfish

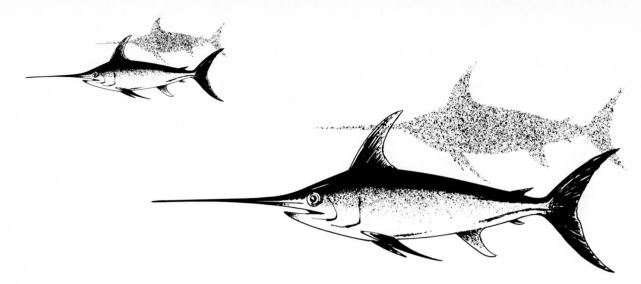

Swordfish

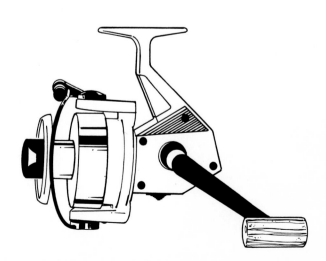

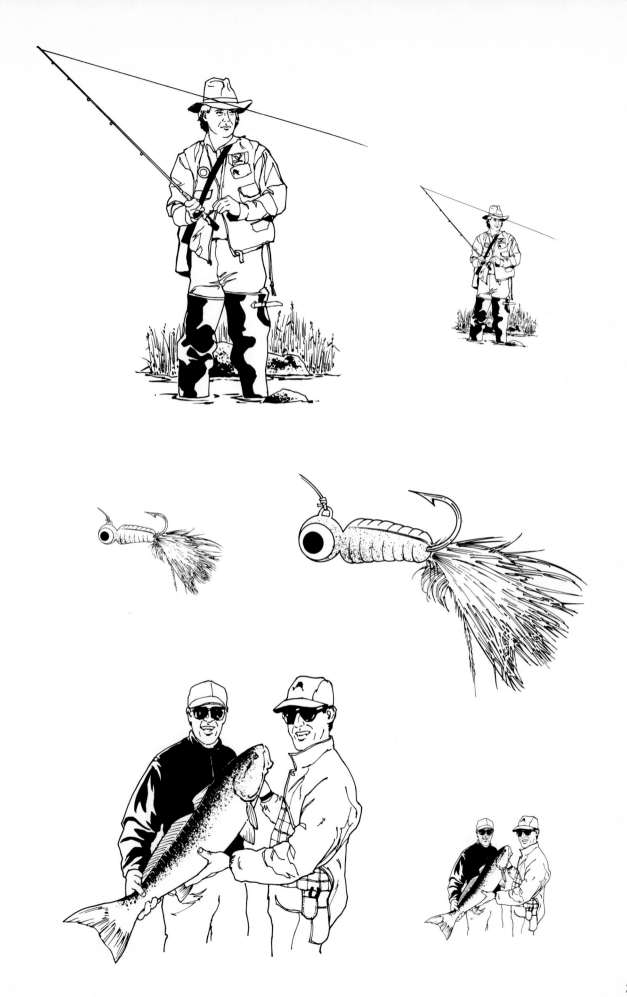

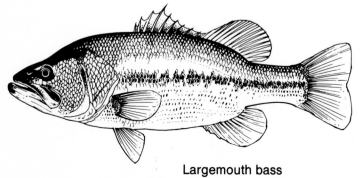

Largemouth bass

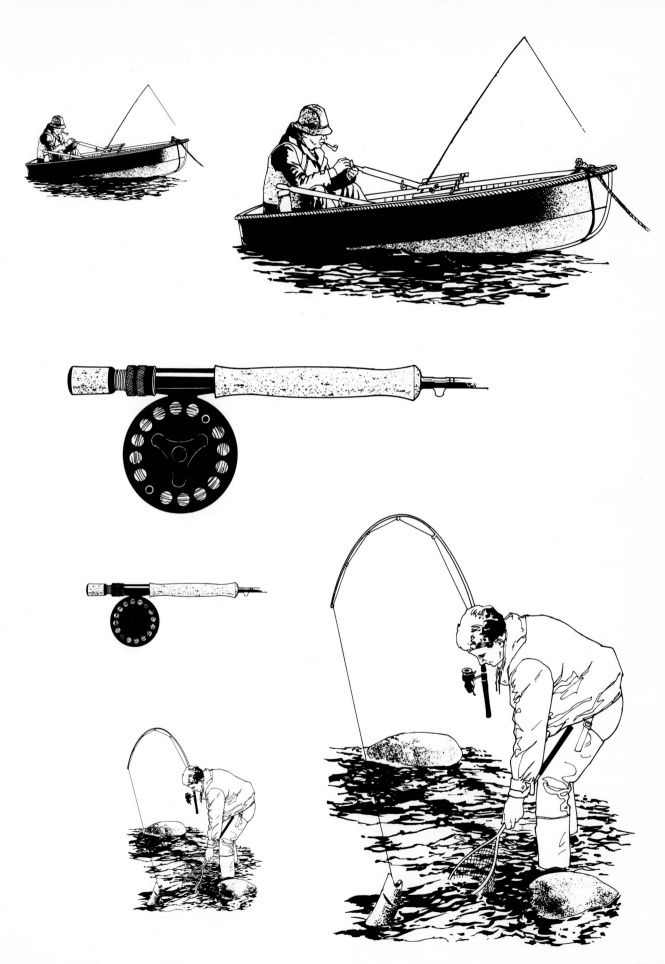

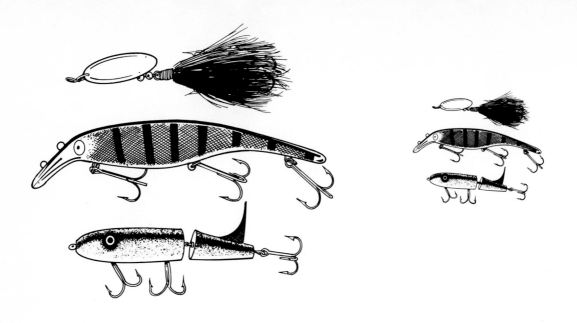

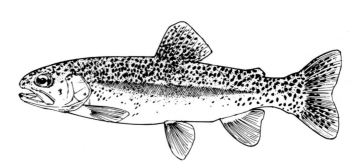

Rainbow trout

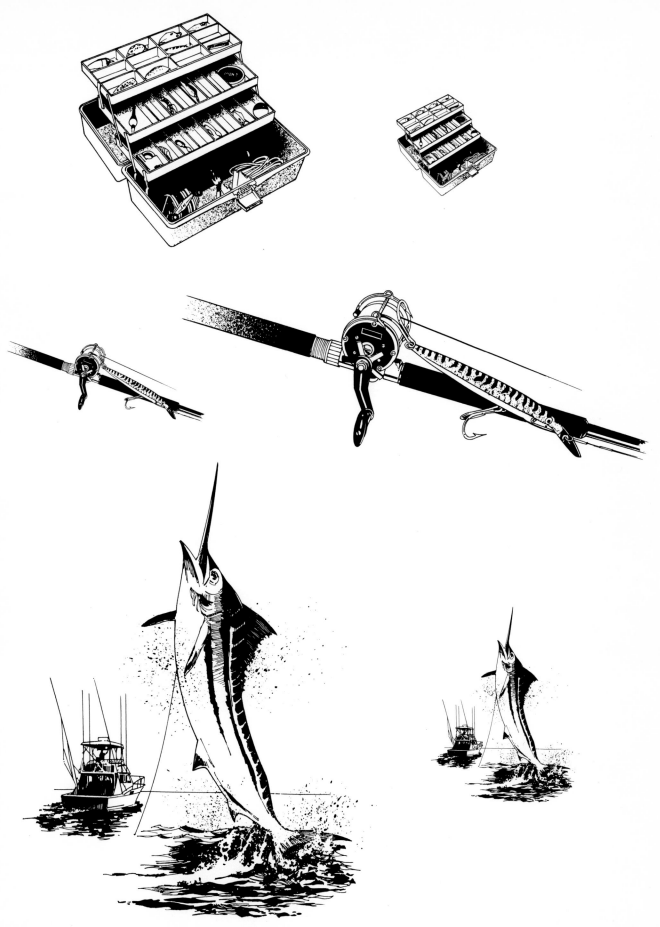

Marlin

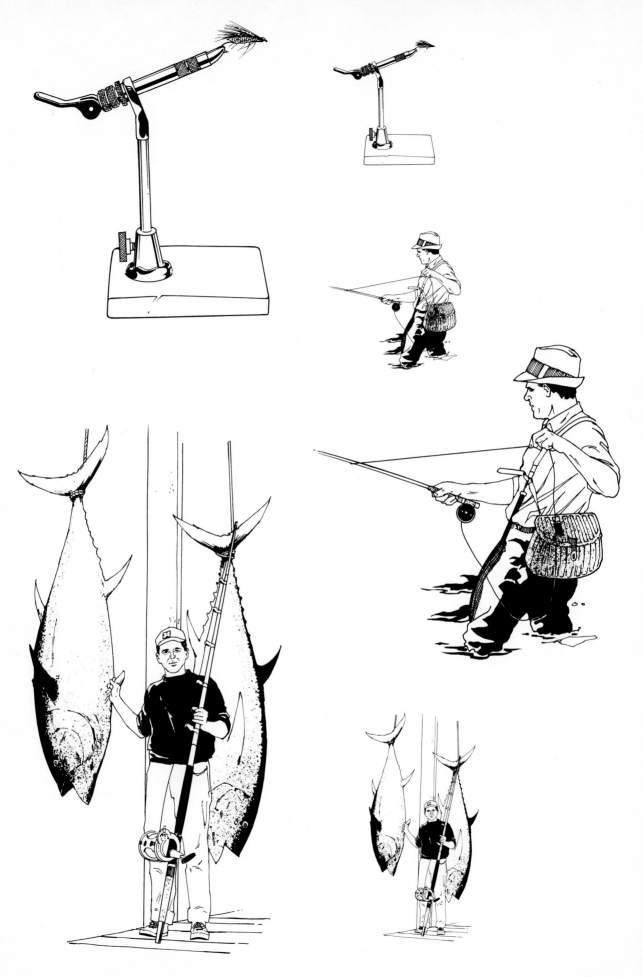

Catfish

Salmon

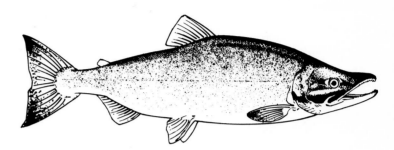
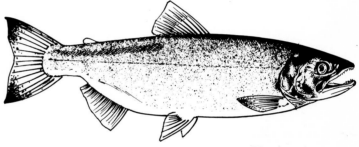

Salmon, old (top) and young adult (bottom)

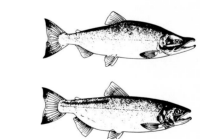